eliminating
stress, finding
inner peace

ALSO BY BRIAN L. WEISS, M.D.

Directing Our Inner Light*

Healing the Mind and Spirit Cards*

Many Lives, Many Masters

Messages from the Masters

Miracles Happen

Mirrors of Time*

Only Love Is Real

Regression Through the Mirrors of Time (audio)*

Regression to Times and Places (audio)*

Same Soul, Many Bodies

Spiritual Progress Through Regression (audio)*

Through Time into Healing

*Available from Hay House

Please visit:

Hay House USA: www.hayhouse.com®
Hay House Australia: www.hayhouse.com.au
Hay House UK: www.hayhouse.co.uk
Hay House India: www.hayhouse.co.in

❋ ❋ ❋

eliminating stress, finding inner peace

BRIAN L. WEISS, M.D.

HAY HOUSE, INC.

Carlsbad, California • New York City

London • Sydney • New Delhi

Published in the United States by: Hay House, Inc.: www.hayhouse.com®
Published in Australia by: Hay House Australia Pty. Ltd.: www.hayhouse.com.au
Published in the United Kingdom by: Hay House UK, Ltd.: www.hayhouse.co.uk
Published in India by: Hay House Publishers India: www.hayhouse.co.in

Cover and Interior design: Julie Davison

The author of this book does not dispense medical advice or prescribe the use of any technique as a form of treatment for physical, emotional, or medical problems without the advice of a physician, either directly or indirectly. The intent of the author is only to offer information of a general nature to help you in your quest for emotional, physical, and spiritual well-being. In the event you use any of the information in this book for yourself, the author and the publisher assume no responsibility for your actions.

Library of Congress Cataloging-in-Publication Data
for the original edition

Weiss, Brian L. (Brian Leslie)
  Eliminating stress, finding inner peace / Brian L. Weiss.
      p. cm.
  ISBN 1-4019-0244-8 (Hardcover)
  1. Stress (Psychology) 2. Stress management. I. Title.
  BF575.S75W44 2003
  155.9'042—dc21

                                                        2003004369

Tradepaper ISBN: 978-1-4019-6162-6
E-book ISBN: 978-1-4019-3221-3

10 9 8 7 6 5 4 3 2
1st edition, September 2003
2nd edition, December 2015
3rd edition, July 2020

Printed in the United States of America

contents

Thank you again for your
Hay House purchase. Enjoy!

Hay House, Inc. • P.O. Box 5100
Carlsbad, CA 92018 • (800) 654-5126

Music by Steven Halpern: "Higher Ground" © 2003. Please visit www.stevenhalpernmusic.com for more information.

Caution: This audio program features meditation/visualization exercises that render it inappropriate for use while driving or operating heavy machinery.

Publisher's note: Hay House products are intended to be powerful, inspirational, and life-changing tools for personal growth and healing. They are not intended as a substitute for medical care. Please use this audio program under the supervision of your care provider. Neither the author nor Hay House, Inc., assumes any responsibility for your improper use of this product.

CHAPTER ONE

the nature of stress

$\mathcal{S}$*tress* seems to be inevitable and omnipresent. Wherever we look, potential sources of stress abound, ready to rob us of our joy and damage our health.

The complexity of modern life has increased our overall levels of stress and tension. Twenty-four-hour television news programs as well as the Internet allow us to learn about tragedies and disasters within moments of their occurrence, no matter where in the world they happen. Advances in transportation and communication technology have allowed for much more mobility in our living and working environments. The extended family has broken down as industries relocate but travel time shortens. There is an illusion of geographical closeness, but parents and grand-parents are not really so close or potentially helpful if they need to board an airplane in order to visit. Just a few decades ago, most extended families still lived in the same town and were available for assistance and support.

There are more single-parent families now, a stressful situation that is exacerbated by the gradual extinction of the extended family. The ominous word *multitasking* hints at the overload we face daily. Information technology is never asleep, as is manifested through cell phones, e-mail, instant messaging, beepers, and other electronic leashes. We cannot get away. There is no "downtime" anymore. Our support systems are eroding, and we are feeling overwhelmed.

Technological advances in warfare and weapons of mass destruction have also increased our level of discomfort. Some negative results of other newer forms of technology, such as nuclear waste, global warming, and environmental poisons, have likewise had a cumulative stress-increasing effect. As the world becomes more complex, we become more stressed. Our spiritual evolution and our ability to recover our healthy homeostasis and equilibrium have simply not progressed at the same rapid rate as these technological stressors.

One effect of these changes has been a shift in the nature and pattern of stress-inducing events. We are now exposed much more frequently to constant or chronic stress. When stressors are relatively acute but infrequent, our bodies have an opportunity to clear the stress hormones and return to more baseline or normal conditions. However, when stressors are as frequent and as pervasive as they seem to be in our modern world, our bodies do not have enough time to reverse the harmful physiological effects. We are constantly bathed in stress hormones, and we pay a huge physical and mental price.

For these reasons, learning to rapidly reduce stress levels, both mentally and physically, is vitally important to maintaining our health in an increasingly overwhelming world. The techniques and the audio download in this book can help you accomplish just that. (Download instructions can be found on page vi.)

* * *

Stress results when we react psychologically and physically to the potential for change in our environment. Our minds react with concern, worry, or fear. Our bodies react by secreting stress chemicals and hormones.

The physiological stress circuit, which existed even in primitive humans as a mechanism to ensure the survival of our species, and which has been genetically refined over many thousands of years, was designed for short-term stressors. A danger is perceived, and the hypothalamus region of our brain responds by releasing CRH (corticotropin-releasing hormone), which activates the pituitary gland to secrete ACTH (adrenocorticotropin), a hormone that causes the adrenal glands to release three additional hormones: epineph-rine (adrenaline), norepinephrine (noradrenaline), and cortisol (glucocorticoid).

Epinephrine and norepinephrine increase blood pressure and cardiac rate, divert blood from the gas-trointestinal system to the muscles, and speed reaction time. Cortisol releases glucose (sugar) from physiolog-ical storage in order to provide immediate fuel to the body. Cortisol also acts to prevent inflammation at the site of potential wounds or injury. The entire circuit of chemical and hormone secretion is known as the hypo-thalamic-pituitary-adrenal (HPA) axis.

A real or imagined threat activates the HPA axis, and we shift to energizing response mode. We are ready to fight or flee, depending on the nature of the danger. Our breathing accelerates, our heart pounds at a rapid rate, and our mind becomes both active and focused at the same time. Our muscles, receiv-ing the increased blood supply and fuel, are ready for immediate action. Our physical strength and agility are enhanced.

In this current world, stress from relationships, financial problems, the evening news, our daily com-mute, or from our work seems to wax and wane but rarely ever ceases. The HPA axis is activated and doesn't really have a well-defined end point. The stress chemicals are chronically secreted. Often we cannot fight, nor can we flee. We feel trapped and impotent. Long-term activation of the HPA axis causes chronic harmful physical and psychological illnesses such as heart disease, ulcers, obesity, substance abuse, depression, immune system suppression, and a host of other medical maladies. Stress reduction not only improves the quality of our lives, it can literally save our lives.

CHAPTER TWO

causes
of stress

Many people are completely oblivious to, or only partially cognizant of, the levels of stress they may be shouldering every day. Many are not aware of the most common causes of stress—stressors that can affect us at any time. *Stress*, in general, can be defined as any activation of the HPA axis, which means almost any stimulus, such as fear or pain, that disturbs or interferes with the normal physiological equilibrium of the individual. Stress is our physiological and psychological response to the daily events in our lives. Smaller stressors of limited duration can be viewed as positive events because our bodies and minds become more alert, focused, energetic, and engaged.

Over brief periods of time, mild to moderate levels of stress can produce beneficial results. For example, since concentration is more focused, actors, musicians, and others find that their performances are often enhanced by this stress-induced effect. Students taking examinations can similarly benefit. In addition to activating the mind and improving concentration, stress hormones increase muscle function and speed reaction time. Athletes and others striving for heightened physical performance can greatly benefit from these psychophysiological changes.

After the mildly stressful event is over, we clear our bodies of the stress hormones and return to our normal state of equilibrium. However, if the stress is too severe or persists over an extended period of time, these beneficial results may be negated.

The following life-changing events are generally considered the most powerful stressors. The effects of these events are cumulative, so if you are subjected to several of these experiences in a relatively short time, you will probably be at a greater risk of developing stress-related symptoms.

- Death of a mate, family member, or close friend

- Suffering a significant injury, illness, or accident

- Loss of a job or severe work problems

- Loss of a significant relationship through divorce or breakup

- Unwanted pregnancy

- Legal problems, especially jail time and lawsuits

- Major financial problems, including being rejected for loans

- Being a victim of crime, violence, or abuse
- Loneliness or betrayal by a loved one
- Traumatic events, such as natural disasters
- Change of residence, job, or marital status
- Becoming a parent
- Problems with children
- Loss of insurance (especially health) or other benefits
- Balancing job and home responsibilities
- Frequent deadlines or unhealthy competition at work or at school
- Domestic disputes
- Issues with fertility
- Retirement
- Perceived failures, criticisms, or humiliation

Of course, there are many other stressors; these are merely some of the more common and potent ones.

CHAPTER THREE

signs and symptoms of stress

$\mathcal{A}s$ I have noted, stress increases secretions of hormones and chemicals in the body that we normally need only in times of emergency. During chronic episodes of stress, heart rhythm is accelerated, blood pressure can increase to dangerous levels, and stomach acidity can erode the lining of our digestive tracts. We feel increasingly miserable and hopeless, and clinical depression can develop. Our sleep is disturbed and unrefreshing, and we feel more and more fatigued and sluggish. Our sexual drive is diminished, affecting our relationships even more. Our weight can balloon up or down, depending upon how our appetite for food is affected.

The economic costs are also considerable. Time lost from work due to stress-related illnesses causes catastrophic losses both to businesses and individuals. The costs to the health-care systems are also staggering. Medical tests, procedures, and even hospitalizations are incredibly expensive and time-consuming. They are also physically unpleasant and can lead to secondary side effects that can be dangerous.

The symptoms of chronic stress may be categorized in many ways. The following divides them into the major categories of psychological, physical, and behavioral.

Psychological Symptoms Include:

- Impaired concentration
- Forgetfulness
- Fears and anxieties
- Depression and other mood disturbances
- Irritability
- Worrying
- Feelings of impending doom
- Low self-esteem
- Being easily distracted
- Anger
- Guilt
- Suspicion
- Getting easily frustrated (low threshold of frustration)
- Loss of motivation; fear of failure

Physical Symptoms Include:

- Headaches
- Increased blood pressure, heart rate
- Sweating
- Tightness of the chest
- Difficulty breathing
- Hyperventilation
- Tremors
- Nervous tics
- Dryness of the mouth and throat
- Feelings of lethargy and fatigue
- Insomnia
- Diarrhea and stomach pains
- Decreased libido
- Obesity or weight loss
- Bruxism (teeth grinding)
- Backaches or neck pain
- Susceptibility to illness

- Palpitations (heart pounding or skipped beats)
- Muscle tightness or tension
- Skin disorders
- Heartburn and acid stomach
- Osteoporosis and bone fractures

Behavioral Symptoms Include:

- Increased use, or resumption of, alcohol, drugs, or tobacco
- Excessive caffeine intake
- Impulsivity
- Aggressive behavior
- Overeating
- Relationship conflicts
- Decreased activity
- Avoidance of people or places; social isolation
- Reappearance or aggravation of phobias
- Withdrawal from responsibility

If you notice that these signs and symptoms are occurring more frequently or with more severity, you may be experiencing increased stress levels. The earlier that stress-reduction techniques are applied, the better you will feel. The negative effects of chronic stress *can* be mitigated. Your body and your mind *can* return to their normal state of function.

CHAPTER FOUR

stress
and illness

$\mathcal{M}any$ medical studies have linked chronic stress to numerous illnesses and problems. In fact, five of the leading causes of death in the United States are linked to stress: heart disease, cancer, lung ailments, cirrhosis of the liver, and suicide. Women are affected as much as men, often more so. Stress respects no particular sex, race, religion, or nationality.

It is well known that stress can impair the functioning of the body's immune system. When immune-system suppression occurs, the body becomes much more vulnerable to infections, both viral and bacterial, as well as to other opportunistic pathogens, such as parasites.

The immune system also plays a major role in impeding many types of cancer. With an impairment or compromise to our immunological defense mechanisms, the ability to ward off or fight cancer cells is correspondingly suppressed, and this can lead to catastrophic consequences. We become more vulnerable to cancer and its spread, and to other chronic medical conditions that interact with our immune system.

It is not just a myth that people who are in love get sick less often. Those in this state tend to be happier and more optimistic. They are not as bothered by the usual stressors in our environments and in our lives. In their transcendent zone of love, they rise above mundane conflicts. When someone is in love, their immune system functions at an optimal level, providing them protection from invading germs, cancer cells, or other attacks on their health.

Stress seems to increase levels of LDL cholesterol, the so-called bad cholesterol linked to increased risks of coronary artery disease. Other studies have demonstrated that sudden mental stress causes the inner layer of blood vessels to constrict, thereby increasing the risk of heart attack or stroke.

The New England Journal of Medicine, widely considered to be the foremost general medical journal in the United States, published a major article in January of 1998 detailing the multi-system damage that chronic stress can inflict on the human body. In addition to heart disease and immune-system dysfunction, the study cited memory loss, insulin resistance, and decreased bone-mineral density (osteoporosis, which leads to weakness of bone and increased likelihood of fractures).

High levels of cortisol can increase appetite and lead to obesity. Prolonged cortisol secretion can trigger increased insulin production. Insulin, a powerful appetite stimulant, also causes increased fat storage, particularly around the waist. In a study at Yale University, women who stored fat primarily in their abdomens were compared to women who stored fat mostly in their hips. The women with abdominal fat reported feeling more threatened by stressful tasks and having more stressful lives. They also produced significantly higher levels of cortisol than the other groups of women. Interestingly, fat cells deep in the waist area are very rich in stress hormone receptors, and a Harvard Medical School study found that abdominal fat was positively correlated with an increased risk of coronary heart disease.

Stress can suppress the reproductive system and impair fertility. The production of the male and female sex hormones, testosterone, estrogen, and progesterone can be inhibited as well. Prolonged HPA axis activation also inhibits the secretion of growth hormone, essential for normal growth.

Numerous studies have linked stress—especially chronic stress—to depression and increased incidences of suicide attempts. These patients also have higher levels of CRH, the hypothalamic stress substance. Other medical and psychological conditions associated with elevated CRH include obsessive-compulsive disorder, anorexia nervosa, several types of anxiety syndromes, alcoholism, diabetes, thyroid disorders, and certain forms of insomnia.

CHAPTER FIVE

posttraumatic stress disorder

Posttraumatic stress is one particular sub-type of stress, an especially powerful and disruptive one that seems to be increasingly common in our violent world. So many of us have been exposed to overwhelming stressors that seem to be out of our control. These traumatic events can be sudden and massive, such as the September 11, 2001, terrorist attacks; or chronically invasive, such as sexual or physical abuse. They can be caused by humans (violence and war); by accidents (fires, airplane or automobile crashes); or by nature (hurricanes, earthquakes, tornadoes). It is our reactions to these events that cause us so much pain and misery, and which tend to be physically and psychologically similar.

Shock, anxiety, guilt, chronic irritability, and depression frequently occur as a result of posttraumatic stress disorder. A high incidence of substance abuse can also result, along with insomnia, nightmares, an exaggerated startle response, and a myriad of psychosomatic disorders. Impairment of concentration; flashbacks; feelings of confusion and despair; low self-esteem; fear of losing control; and the persistent, intrusive fear that the traumatic event or events will recur are also common. Finally, posttraumatic reactions have a significant association with certain psychiatric disorders.

Researchers estimate that 40 to 60 percent of women treated for serious eating disorders such as anorexia and bulimia have memories of traumas in their pasts. In one research study, among crime victims with posttraumatic stress, 41 percent experienced sexual dysfunction, 82 percent had depression, 27 percent manifested obsessive-compulsive symptoms, and 18 percent suffered from phobias.

About 25 to 30 percent of individuals witnessing or experiencing a traumatic event will exhibit significant symptoms of posttraumatic stress disorder. Without treatment, 50 percent of these people will suffer for decades from these symptoms. Time, by itself, is not the perfect healer.

The statistics regarding stress-related events and costs are truly alarming. A 1996 *Prevention* magazine survey found that 75 percent of Americans experience "great stress" at least once weekly, and 33 percent report feeling this way more than twice a week. A consensus of research surveys estimates that 75 to 90 percent of all visits to primary-care physicians are for stress-related problems. One million employees are absent on an average workday due to stress-related symptoms. Seventy-eight percent of Americans describe their jobs as being stressful, and stress costs American industries approximately $300 billion annually. Sixty to eighty percent of accidents on the job are related to stress, and violent workplace incidents are frequently caused by this condition. Data from Canada and the United Kingdom indicate very similar statistics. Stress, obviously, knows no boundaries.

Because most physicians do not have the time or resources to help discover and eliminate the sources

of the stress, they often prescribe medication—often multiple medications—to treat their patients. All drugs have side effects, potentially worsening problems rather than alleviating them. Many medicines used for treating stress and anxiety are addicting, further exacerbating the condition. It seems as if we are constantly shuttling between the frying pan and the fire.

For many years, physicians have been prescribing anxiolytic drugs, especially the benzodiazepines (Valium, Librium, Xanax, Tranxene, Dalmane, Serax, Ativan, and so on) for symptoms of anxiety or insomnia. These medicines, differentiated primarily by how

long they linger in the body, frequently produce side effects such as drowsiness, decreased energy, dry mouth, constipation, impairment of coordination, and mental confusion. They are also habit-forming, and withdrawal from these medicines must be carefully monitored. Usually they are tapered off very gradually to prevent an abstinence syndrome.

Antidepressant medicines have been widely utilized to treat various types of depression. At first, the tricyclic antidepressants (Elavil, Tofranil, Sinequan, Pamelor, Norpramin, and so on) were the most commonly used. Because of the high incidence of side

effects, however, these antidepressants have been supplanted by a newer generation of mood-elevating medicines that work primarily on the serotonin system. These antidepressants (such as Prozac, Paxil, Celexa, Effexor, and Zoloft) have fewer side effects, yet enough to cause significant discomfort or noncompliance nevertheless.

Medications to treat symptoms of anxiety and depression can be a valuable adjunctive treatment, but all medicines cause side effects that must be monitored. In general, the use of medicines without concomitant training in relaxation techniques, and without the insight and understanding that therapy or meditation can provide, will not yield the greatest effectiveness.

Traditional treatments such as individual or group psychotherapy have always been useful in alleviating symptoms of stress. Obviously these techniques require the participation of a well-trained therapist. In addition to the understanding that therapy provides, learning effective communication skills will transfer to other interpersonal encounters and will promote more effective, supportive interactions. The feeling of social isolation diminishes, enhancing self-esteem and further facilitating the therapeutic process. Support groups provide similar advantages and healing opportunities.

I still prescribe medications, particularly antidepressants, for some of my patients because these drugs can elevate mood and improve concentration. However, I always combine their use with meditation, self-relaxation, and stress-reduction practices. This allows me to use the medicines in lower dosages and for a far shorter duration. I have noticed that patients do much better when combining stress reduction and medication than with drugs alone. They also feel more empowered and more in control, because they are learning techniques and approaches that will minimize future episodes, both in severity and duration.

Just about all of my patients use relaxation and stress-reduction exercises, such as those on the audio accompanying this book.

If you are currently in therapy or using prescription drugs, do not alter your medication regimen or therapy schedule without discussing these matters with your physician or therapist.

CHAPTER SIX

a few clinical cases

Considerable medical research has been conducted in the field of psychoneuroimmunology—the mind/body connection—in particular, the effects of stress reduction on the immune system. For example, studies at the University of Miami have shown that maintaining an optimistic attitude is positively correlated with optimal adjustment and less distress during the period following breast cancer surgery. Relaxation training and other stress-management techniques employed over a ten-week period after the surgery resulted in improved psychological and biological functioning. These improvements lasted up to one year or longer after the ten-week trial period ended. The women who participated in the stress-reduction and relaxation protocol showed decreases in depression, "an increased sense of meaning in life, improved social relationships, and a general re-prioritizing of life matters."

According to Dr. Michael Antoni, the director of the Center for Psycho-Oncology Research at the Sylvester Comprehensive Cancer Center at the University of Miami:

> In parallel with these psychological changes, we have observed that . . . participants show decreases in adrenal "stress" hormones such as

cortisol. These cortisol reductions were greatest in women who reported the largest psychological changes. . . . Reductions in cortisol may be important for women with breast cancer, as elevated cortisol levels are associated with decreases in several aspects of immune system functioning. This is relevant since immune surveillance of new cancer cells may protect against the development of metastatic disease.

A patient of mine, a woman in her 40s who had breast cancer and a subsequent lumpectomy, could not tolerate chemotherapy because of overwhelming and disabling side effects. We practiced deep relaxation techniques and healing visualizations, and her threshold for pain and discomfort was altered by these practices. She learned to concentrate very deeply and learned how to shut out the discomfort of chemotherapy. Her oncologist was then able to raise her dosage into the therapeutic range, and her cancer went into remission.

Did the remission result from the chemotherapy, from the relaxation techniques and the healing visualization exercises, or from the combination? It really doesn't matter. She improved dramatically, and remains well 14 years after the initial surgery.

* * *

Medical-research studies on cardiac disease have found that a combination of moderate exercise, proper diet, and the practice of stress-reduction techniques can actually *reverse* blockages in coronary artery disease. Interestingly, when diet and exercise regimens were followed, but a stress-reduction approach was not practiced, there was a diminution in the progression of the heart disease, but the coronary blockages were *not* reversed. When stress-reduction techniques were added, a real reversal of the cardiac damage occurred.

Studies such as these provide profound implications for the role of stress-reduction practices in the prevention and the *reversal* of serious medical illnesses. If reversal of illness can occur, then it is never too late to begin learning techniques to minimize and eliminate stress.

Several years ago, a prominent cardiologist referred one of his patients to me. The year before, the patient had suffered a severe heart attack. Ed was only 51 years old. Because the cardiac damage was extensive, the leisure activities he liked to engage in were mostly forbidden now. He loved to scuba dive, but his cardiologist prohibited him from diving because of underwater pressure gradients. Ed was an avid deep-sea boater and fisherman, but his cardiologist restricted this, too, concerned that Ed might be too far from a hospital in case the need for emergency treatment arose.

Ed was understandably anxious about another myocardial infarction because he barely had enough cardiac function to live. He tired quickly when walking. Previously a heavy smoker, he considered resuming his smoking habit to relieve his omnipresent anxiety. Ed was becoming more and more depressed, and he had a sense of impending doom. Small stressors were magnified, both at home and at work. He was short-tempered with his wife and his colleagues at work, and they were becoming more and more frustrated with him. The antianxiety medicines his doctors had prescribed were not really helping. His cardiac medications seemed only to stem the tide. He was not recuperating well at all. When I first saw him, Ed was a wreck.

We began therapy, scheduling weekly sessions in my office. I gave Ed a stress-reduction CD and asked him to use it daily at home. He began using the CD twice daily, rather quickly mastering the physical-relaxation component. Soon he even began light exercise on a stationary bicycle, pedaling as he listened to the CD. When he finished exercising, he'd listen again.

Within weeks, Ed's exercise tolerance had noticeably increased. Within months, his cardiac disease had begun to reverse. His anxiety had virtually disappeared, and the urge to smoke had vanished. His relationships at home and at work dramatically improved.

Ed's cardiologist was amazed at his progress and lifted the boating restrictions. He began to refer many of his patients to me, looking for similar miracles. But I knew that Ed's progress was not a miracle. By practicing diligently, he had learned how to enter a deep level of relaxation, how to eliminate stress and anxiety, and how to allow the natural healing power of his body and mind to cure his illness.

Today Ed remains in excellent health, without any recurrence of his previously progressive coronary artery disease. A significant portion of his heart muscle has regenerated. In addition, he has been able to achieve and maintain a sense of inner peace and calm in his everyday consciousness, even when he's not meditating or practicing with the CD. His perspective about life—what is important and what is not—has changed for the better. He is much happier now.

* * *

Smoking cessation is another important area that benefits from the practice of stress-reduction techniques. It is not necessary to enumerate the harmful effects of primary and secondhand tobacco use. Lung cancer, emphysema, heart disease, and premature aging of the skin are only a few of the serious medical consequences of chronic smoking. In helping smokers kick the habit, the success rate of stress-reduction techniques is significant. Not only are people freed of their addictions, but the health benefits are enormous, both to the smoker and to those around them.

CHAPTER SEVEN

stress and worry

There are innumerable sources of stress stemming from events that we cannot control. But we *do* have control over our reactions to these events. Unfortunately, we spend more time worrying than we do trying to gain understanding and perspective.

We have so many worries. We worry about money, yet we know that money is only a tool, a means to an end. What we really want is happiness, a bit of security in our lives, some modicum of joy. Happiness, security, and joy are inner states. They are free; money cannot purchase them. Worry is merely a habit—and a negative, unpleasant habit at that. Worry will not change anything, nor will it bring you those things that you really need and desire. And money will not bring you happiness. I have treated many extremely wealthy people in my psychotherapy practice, and many of them have been miserable and unhappy. Money is a neutral thing, neither good nor bad. What you do with money creates its value.

We worry about success and failure, yet we cannot really define these concepts. Is a poor person who is happy and who has wonderful, loving relationships a failure? Is a rich person who has terrible relationships and no love in his life a success? Our cultures have defined success and failure for us, and the definitions have been deficient. So what is the point in worrying about success?

We worry too much about what other people think of us—about their opinions, judgments, and criticisms. Yet their opinions are based on the same cultural values as those measuring money and defining success. Once again, we are worrying about nothing.

All other apprehensions fall into the same paradigm. Worrying cannot effect positive change or growth. It will not change the future. Planning for the future is useful, but worrying is not. This is a useless

habit, a conditioned response we have acquired from our parents, our teachers, and our communities. Intellectually we all know this, but old habits are difficult to break. If we could only stop worrying so much, how much happier we all would be! We would experience much less stress in our lives.

The irony is that, when observed from a more detached perspective, this type of stress is an illusion. It is not real. We create it ourselves. And we all know this.

Events or perceptions that have the capacity to induce stress reactions in us are subjective and relative. An occurrence that traumatizes you may not affect me at all, or vice versa. An event that caused you considerable stress last year may hardly register this year, because your attitude or perspective may have changed in that period of time. You may even enjoy the experience this time around or perceive it as an exciting challenge rather than a threat, trauma, or stressor. It is quite simply all in the eye of the beholder. Our free will determines our reaction to these events. Will we react with fear, or with confidence and optimism? The choice is ours to make: stress or confidence, fear or love, anxiety or inner peace.

※ ※ ※

I have been a guest on hundreds of television shows in many countries. Now, I rarely become anxious about appearing on even the most popular national programs, yet I still vividly remember the anxiety I felt before appearing on television the very first time. It was on a small local program that, on a good night, hardly anyone watched. My heart was palpitating. My voice, I am sure, was shaky. My hands trembled. What changed?

Well, the only difference was my understanding. On that night, I was concerned with how I looked; how I sounded; what people, especially my friends

and family, would think; and how my colleagues would regard me. With time and experience, I have come to see my role as a teacher, not a performer. What I have to say is much more important than how I look. I try to present what I have learned and what my patients and workshop participants have taught me so the viewer can share in the knowledge. I am no longer concerned with what the host or my friends think, as long as I am really trying my best to teach and help others. As soon as I realized that this was my purpose, anxiety and stress melted away.

CHAPTER EIGHT

stress and spirituality

Believing in a divine plan or purpose can drastically reduce stress. We need to look for lessons, things to be learned, from the obstacles in our lives. Sometimes the lifetimes with the most obstacles are those in which we can make the most spiritual progress, where we learn our soul lessons at an accelerated pace. To look for the lesson in an obstacle, or even in a tragedy, allows us to discern the purpose in the event. When we understand the lesson, we can choose to let go of pain and suffering.

As Christian mystic Pierre Teilhard de Chardin once said: "We are not human beings having a spiritual experience; we are spiritual beings having a human experience." He was right. If we recognize the soul lesson, we can grow beyond suffering, and there is no stress in this state of understanding.

We are overly attached to the results of our actions. If we would detach from our obsession to outcomes, to our assessments of success or failure, we would feel so much happier. If we could only reach out to others with love and compassion and not be concerned with what comes back to us—what we will or will not *gain*—our lives would be filled with joy.

Love is the antidote to stress—yet in this violent, greedy, and hate-filled world, it seems so difficult to love unconditionally. This is an extremely challenging spiritual lesson. If you could love unconditionally . . . if you were ever mindful of your true spiritual nature, of your soul . . . if you expected no return for your unsolicited compassionate actions . . . if you could let go of your emotional attachments to material things . . . then you would never again experience prolonged or unhealthy stress in your life, and your days and nights would be filled with happiness and joy.

Very few, if any of us, enter this life in a state of spiritual enlightenment. As a psychiatrist, I am aware

of the huge struggle to overcome familial and cultural conditioning. How can we be spiritually mindful when our subconscious and unconscious conditioning create sinkholes and quicksand to trap our minds? One way is to start at the beginning.

a threefold approach to stress reduction

The exercise on the audio included in this book approaches the alleviation of stress in three ways: physical, psychological, and spiritual.

The first approach is physical, achieved by helping the body reach a profound state of muscular relaxation. If you practice this exercise regularly, you will find that you are able to reach a deeper and deeper level of relaxation and inner peace, each time more and more quickly and easily. As you learn how to totally relax key muscle groups in your body, a kind of muscle memory is established. In addition, an awareness of levels of muscle tension is developed and fine-tuned, and you will quickly become aware of subtle changes in the degree of muscle tension much earlier than usual. The relaxation techniques can then be carried into everyday life and, in times of stress, used consciously, breaking the cycle of muscle tension and physical symptoms.

The physical antidote to the stress reaction is extremely important. By practicing with the audio, or by utilizing other relaxation and meditative techniques, you can abort the production of stress hormones and transmitters. Your body will quickly restore its normal nonstress equilibrium as the stress chemicals are neutralized. By practicing, you can become quite expert at blocking the stress reaction altogether.

The audio will teach you how to control your breathing and to completely prevent hyperventilating. When a person breathes too rapidly, an excess amount of carbon dioxide is exhaled, and oxygen consumption is likewise increased. This process leads to feelings of light-headedness, faintness, and anxiety. Most panic attacks are accompanied and exacerbated by hyperventilation. These attacks can be aborted by relaxing skeletal muscles, ending the hyperventilating. Early level of awareness or mindfulness is critical to the cessation of the stress reaction or anxiety attack, because the "rescue remedies" can be instituted immediately.

The old technique of breathing into a brown paper bag to terminate an anxiety attack is based on the same principle. As the air is re-breathed, it becomes richer in carbon dioxide and the oxygen content drops, restoring a more normal equilibrium. Of course, with early awareness that you are beginning to hyperventilate, the paper bag becomes unnecessary.

When you learn how to control your breathing and your musculature, you can find that place of deep peace and security that is always within. When you reach this level of inner peace, you can completely cease the production of any stress chemicals or hormones. You have mastered your body and your mind. You are in control. At this level, nobody and no thing can rob you of your inner peace and joy.

When mystics master this state, they describe how they are freed from fear, stress, desire, and the control of others. They can be in jail or prison, yet they are completely free. We are all mystics. We can all be free. We just have to remember how.

The second approach is psychological. The script makes the listener aware of the nature of stress, about its causes and cures. The harmful effects of stress upon the body and the psyche are emphasized, along with the understanding that we *can* learn to consciously let go of stress by changing our attitudes, perceptions, and perspective. The listener is empowered by the knowledge that we have *control* over stress-inducing situations. When we choose, we can alter our mental state and conditioning. We can transform stress into a positive life lesson.

* * *

Another patient of mine, a 35-year-old insurance executive, disliked his job intensely, but he felt trapped because his position brought him a great deal of wealth and prestige. Although Jay had a large, beautiful house and an expensive sports car, his marriage was disintegrating, and he was in the midst of hostile divorce proceedings. He felt stressed at work and at home. Insomnia, gastrointestinal distress, headaches, and lethargy were plaguing his life. He was beginning to have anxiety attacks.

Our therapeutic approach was the threefold model discussed previously—the physical, psychological, and spiritual. We actively utilized the relaxation response, and Jay religiously practiced with the stress reduction audio. He rapidly learned how to relax his muscles and how to control his breathing in order to prevent hyperventilating when under stress.

The concept of mindfulness or awareness is critical in this process. Mindfulness means total awareness of all that is happening in the present moment, awareness of what your muscles are doing, what thoughts and emotions are present in your mind *at this very moment in time*, and what you are perceiving. When you are mindful, you minimize anxiety, because you have become the objective observer of your physical and mental processes.

As soon as Jay became aware of an increase in tension or tightness of his muscles, he began to relax them. As soon as he recognized that he was hyperventilating, he consciously slowed his respiratory rate.

The psychological approach with Jay involved an expanded perception, and an understanding of himself and the stressors in his life. He began to realize that other people's opinions and impressions did not need to affect him negatively or to diminish his self-esteem. Others' opinions were subjective, based on their own enculturation and experiences. Jay knew that he was a good person, empathetic and compassionate, and the opinions and thoughts of others did not by themselves have the power to rob him of his inner peace or joy. Only he could let them do this, and now he disempowered the negative and critical people in his life.

Jay also realized that authentic security is an inner state. We can lose our material possessions at any time, but only we can give away our inner peace, our self-esteem, and self-love. Jay's house, car, bank accounts, and boat were just possessions, just things. They did not measure him as a person. His compassionate actions, his thoughts and deeds, and his emotional and spiritual evolution were much more important. He understood spiritually that we do not take our material things with us when we die. We take our relationships, our learning, our growth.

Jay understood that the quality of his relationships was more important than the quantity of his possessions. His divorce was amicable. He and his wife realized that they had grown apart in many ways, as people often do. They were able to communicate clearly and with caring as they freed each other to grow along their different paths.

Jay realized that he had a facility for writing, a passion he had abandoned many years earlier because he had been erroneously taught that money was more important than his dreams. He closed his office and moved to California, where he achieved considerable success as a screenwriter. He is much happier now.

* * *

The third approach is the spiritual one. As we truly understand the nature of our souls and the lessons we all came here to learn; as we remember that we are immortal, eternal, then not only is stress released, but an energy of joy and love flows into our awareness like a river being renewed by the refreshing rains of spring.

It is not necessary to master all three approaches in order to benefit from the audio. Acquiring the skills of deep physical relaxation will, in itself, produce healing relief. The somatic symptoms of stress will be released. Your body will feel better, your energy level will increase, your sleep will improve and become more refreshing, and you will feel more inner peace. You will have gained the ability to quell the symptoms of stress and anxiety when they arise, and you will have learned how to restore your body to a peaceful equilibrium.

You can prevent the stress or anxiety from progressing to uncomfortable or dangerous levels. You will find that you are in control of your physical body.

Similarly, your physical health will benefit. Clearly, symptoms of stress such as headaches, stomach hyperacidity, elevated blood pressure, cardiac problems, insomnia and nightmares, weight gain or loss, hair loss, skin disorders, anxiety and panic attacks, difficulty concentrating, chronically low energy levels, and a host of other medical problems will significantly diminish or even be eliminated. We all possess an amazing ability to influence and control the physiological processes of our bodies. We have mostly forgotten how to master these processes, but we can regain these skills with practice. The audio download included with this book will teach you how.

As you feel more and more in control of your physical state, your mental outlook will brighten, and you will feel more optimistic and hopeful. Your mood will improve as feelings of sadness or hopelessness lessen. As your mood lightens, your relationships with other people will also be enhanced, because you will react more positively and patiently. Others will sense your happier, more peaceful attitude, and their reactions to you will similarly improve. A positive cycle of improved interaction in your relationships will be established and maintained because it is self-reinforcing.

In my fourth book, *Messages from the Masters: Tapping into the Power of Love,* I wrote about how to remove obstacles to our happiness and joy. Spiritual understanding can dissolve stress and fear; our perspective can be shifted from the everyday and ordinary to the transcendent and timeless. As this shift in consciousness occurs, stress can be eliminated. We see and feel the world in a different way. I wrote:

> We are all created in the image of God and God is within us all. Our basic underlying nature is loving, peaceful, balanced, and harmonious. We are innately compassionate, caring, and kind. We are souls.
>
> Over the course of our lifetimes, an overlay of fear, anger, envy, sadness, insecurity, and many other negative thoughts and emotions accrues and covers our beautiful inner nature. This outer covering is intensified and reinforced by our childhood training and experiences in the current life. We appear to be what we are not—angry and fearful people, filled

with insecurity, guilt, and self-doubts. We have forgotten who we really are.

We do not need to learn about love and balance, about peace and compassion, about forgiveness and faith. We have always known these things.

Instead, our task is to *unlearn* those negative and harmful emotions and attitudes that plague our lives and cause us, our communities, and our world such misery. As we let go of these negative traits, lo and behold, we rediscover our true nature, our positive and

loving self. It has been there all the time, covered over, obscured, and forgotten.

When we remove the outer layers of dirt and debris, the negative thoughts and emotions, when we clean and polish away the outer overlay, then we can once again discern the true diamonds we really are. We are immortal and divine souls on our way home. We have always been diamonds underneath. . . .

To let go of negative thoughts and emotions and to discover inner peace, joy, and happiness—these are the goals. You will find life so much more enjoyable. You will progress with more awareness along your spiritual path. And your soul will manifest itself within a physical body that is infinitely more healthy and resistant to diseases. What a wonderful combination. Even if you are still debating or mulling over the spiritual lessons and implications, there is no doubt about the physical benefits you can obtain from the practices and attitudes described here. These health benefits present strong practical reasons for following the suggestions. . . . Along the way, spiritual benefits will accrue anyway. You have nothing to lose, and you have everything to gain.

CHAPTER TEN

how to use the audio

The stress-reduction exercise on the accompanying audio is a powerful tool for self-healing. It teaches techniques to achieve profound states of relaxation. It will instruct you how to recognize and release muscle tension and tightness. Awareness and control of respiratory rhythm is learned. Mindfulness of physical, emotional, and psychological perceptions is attained and used as a device to achieve a level of healthy equilibrium whenever desired.

The audio is perfectly safe. You are instructed that if you are ever uncomfortable with any image or feeling, you can detach and float above, observing or feeling from a distance. If you are still uncomfortable, you can return to a beautiful and peaceful scene, or you can open your eyes at any time and end the process. You are always in control.

In actuality, discomfort while listening to the audio is extremely rare. The overwhelming effect is one of peace and deep relaxation. Stress and anxiety diminish and often disappear. The audio never creates symptoms; it heals them.

This stress-reduction audio can be a valuable aid in reducing anxiety, improving mood, and healing symptoms. However, it is not intended to be a substitute for medical or psychological care, although it can certainly be used in conjunction with other therapeutic techniques. If you are dealing with any significant mental or emotional disorder, are undergoing psychotherapy, are experiencing seizures, or have any neurological illness, consult your physician or therapist first and only use the audio under his or her supervision.

You will experience benefits at many levels, including the physical, emotional, psychological, and

spiritual. You may become aware of positive changes after the first time or two, or you may need more practice, which is why patience may be necessary. Sometimes other people become aware of positive transformation in you even before you become aware of it. The key is to avoid frustration and keep practicing. There is no magic formula. The more you practice, the deeper and deeper you will go, ever more quickly, until you reach that beautiful level of inner peace and tranquility where change and transformation occur.

appendix

Stress-Reduction Audio Transcript

Let us begin by closing your eyes and taking a few relaxing breaths: breathing out stress, tension, tightness; breathing in beautiful energy. And as you do this, you will find your body relaxing more and more with each breath. Use your imagination. Imagine that you can actually breathe *out* the stresses and the tensions that you store in your body, and that you can breathe *in* the beautiful energy, which is all around you. And there really is.

And as you do this—breathing out stress, breathing out tension—you will find your body relaxing more and more with each breath. And as you do this, allow your muscles to completely relax.

Relax completely the muscles of your face and your jaw, letting go of all tightness and all tension in these muscles. Sometimes people who have jaw problems, headaches, neck pains, are clenching their teeth too tightly as a result of stress. So just let your face, your jaw, completely relax.

And now completely relax the muscles of your neck, letting go of all tightness and all tension in these muscles. Feel your neck, so soft, so relaxed, as you go deeper and deeper into a beautiful state of peace and calm and serenity. And this is very *healthy* for you— healthy for your body and healthy for your mind—to relax completely, to let go of tensions, stresses, tightness. To feel the beautiful peace that is always around you and within you. And so you go deeper and deeper relaxed with each breath.

And as you do this now, completely relax the muscles of your shoulders. People who carry too much responsibility often feel a tightness, a tension, in their shoulders. Let your shoulders completely relax.

And now completely relax the muscles of your back—both the upper back and the lower back—letting go of all tension. People who have back pain often tense these muscles because of stress. And so let your back muscles completely relax. Let go of these tensions. Allow yourself to go even deeper. This is very safe . . . as you go even deeper.

You'll be able to follow my voice. And let my voice carry you deeper and deeper relaxed, but let other distractions or noises or thoughts only deepen your level even more as they fade away. You can go deep enough now.

And next, completely relax the muscles of your arms. So soft, so loose. And now completely relaxing the muscles of your stomach and your abdomen so that your breathing stays perfectly relaxed as you go even deeper . . . even deeper.

And now completely relax the muscles of your legs so that your whole body is now going deeper and deeper into a beautiful state of peace and calm and serenity. And this state is so healthy for you—for your body, for your mind—to relax, to let go of tensions and stresses, to find that inner peace, to go within. This is so healthy for you. And so you can let yourself go even deeper now.

And as you stay in this beautiful state of peace and calm, of relaxation, of tranquility; as you feel the peace all around you and within you, know that you have the ability to let go of stress and tension. You have the ability to relax whenever you want, whenever you need, just by focusing on these muscles, allowing them to completely relax, by following your breath, your breathing. Breathing out stresses and tensions, breathing in beautiful energy, and going deeper and deeper with each breath into this beautiful state of peace and calm and tranquility.

You always have this power, this ability. Whenever you need to, whenever you want to. To relax, to go within, to break the cycle of stress and tension before it even begins. To control your breathing so that your breathing remains calm and peaceful. To relax your muscles, and to find that state of inner calm, which is so beautiful and so important to you.

Imagine now that there is a beautiful light above your head. This is a healing light, a relaxing light, a deepening light. You can choose the color or colors of this beautiful light. This is a healing light because as it flows down your body, it will heal—getting rid of illness, disease, and discomfort—every organ, every fiber, every cell of your body. This is a deepening light because it will bring you to a deeper and deeper level of peace and calm and serenity. This is a spiritual light, connected to the light above and around you.

And let the light come into your body now through the top of your head, illuminating your brain, healing the brain, the spinal cord, and flowing down from above to below like a beautiful wave of light. And the light flows all the way into your heart, your beautiful heart, healing your heart and allowing the beautiful energy of your heart to flow throughout your body, bringing healing relief everywhere.

And the light fills up all of the abdominal organs as well, healing these—getting rid of illness, disease, and discomfort—and restoring to perfect health. The light fills all of the muscles and nerves and bones of your body, your back—everywhere—bringing relief, bringing healing . . . allowing you to go even deeper. Let the light be very strong, very powerful, wherever *you* need it for healing. The light dissolves stress and tension and returns your body to the normal, healthy state. The light heals the lining of your digestive system, of your stomach . . . healing this. It relaxes the muscles and nerves of your body even more. It helps your heart to function beautifully, normally. It repairs your blood pressure, and it repairs any illness, disease, or stress-related consequences of tension. It restores your body to perfect health. And also your mind—because the light helps to dissolve fear, anxieties, worries. The light helps you to get rid of sadness and guilt and anger. The light is so peaceful, so beautiful, so healing. Let it fill your body now; let it be very strong and very powerful wherever you need it for healing. Feel the light in these areas of your body or your mind that need healing.

And let the rest of the light flow down both legs, until it reaches all the way to your feet, filling your body with this beautiful healing light. Let yourself go even deeper now. It is perfectly safe.

And next, visualize or imagine that the light also completely surrounds the outside of your body as well—as if you were wrapped in a beautiful bubble or cocoon of light, wrapping around you, protecting you completely, healing your skin and the outer muscles, and deepening your level even more.

In a few moments, I will count backward from ten to one. With each number down, let yourself go deeper and deeper relaxed . . . so deep that the usual boundaries of space and time disappear. So deep that you can bring healing, relaxation, complete peace to every part of your body and your mind. So deep that you can remember every experience you have ever had. So deep that you can experience all levels of your beautiful, multidimensional self, because you are far, far greater than your body *or* your brain. You are a beautiful, immortal, eternal, multidimensional being—filled with light, with love, with peace. And you are always loved, always protected. You can never be harmed—not at this level. Ten, nine, eight—going deeper and deeper with each number back—seven, six, five—deeper and deeper and deeper—four . . . three—a beautiful level of peace, calm, serenity—two . . . one. Good.

In this beautiful state of peace, of calm, imagine now that you're walking down a beautiful staircase: Down, down, deeper and deeper, down, down, deeper and deeper, each step down deepening your level even more. Down, down, deeper and deeper. And as you reach the bottom of the steps, in front of you is a beautiful garden. A garden of peace, joy, light, love, and complete safety. A sanctuary for you, a haven. The garden is filled with beautiful flowers and plants.

And imagine now that you go into this beautiful garden and you find a place to rest. Here your body—still filled with the light and surrounded by the light—continues to heal; to relax; to let go of all tension, stress, tightness; to repair; to heal; to rejuvenate. And the deepest, deepest levels of your mind can open up. You can remember everything. You can heal your body and your mind: You have this power.

Imagine now that a beautiful spiritual being, like a guide or an angel or a master, comes to visit you in this garden. This is someone who's very, very wise, very loving. Perhaps there are more than one. And imagine that you can communicate, whether through words or thoughts or feelings or visions or mind-to-mind contact, or in any other way. You can communicate. Are there any messages for you? Any wisdom, any information, any knowledge, that you can bring back with you? Knowledge and wisdom that will help you now to remove any obstacles to your inner peace and joy and happiness? Knowledge that will increase your perspective and allow you to keep a state of inner peace and calm whenever you wish? Knowledge that will bring you more joy, more happiness, more understanding, in your current life in the current time? Are there any messages for you? Just listen. Just feel. Feel the love, feel the peace, feel the wisdom.

And your beautiful friend or friends are going to take you on a journey of healing. And so you feel your body becoming very, very light as you float above the garden. And you can travel across vast distances of space and time. And you and your friend travel until you come to a beautiful and ancient island—an island of healing, of restoration, of peace—and you find yourself walking on the beautiful beach of this island. The sun is so pleasant and so warm.

Embedded in the floor of the sea, a little ways out from the beach, are several large and powerful ancient healing crystals. And these crystals impart a healing energy to the water so that this water is supercharged with healing energy. And if you wish, if you are comfortable, go into the water a little bit or more. Immediately you feel it tingling. The water is so powerful, so charged with healing energy. You can even breathe in this water, it is so powerful. And the healing energy from the crystals imparted to the water—felt as this beautiful tingling and healing energy—is absorbed by your body, through your skin, into whatever part of your body or your mind needs healing. Feel the power of the water. If you are uncomfortable in water, just stay on the beach, feeling the powerful healing rays of the sun, the intense and beautiful relaxation.

But if you are in the water, then imagine now— visualize—that some beautiful and tame and very loving dolphins come to swim with you for a while. Dolphins are master healers; they know just where in your body or your mind that healing needs to take place. And these dolphins help the beautiful healing water to be even more powerful, even more effective, to heal you—to restore to perfect health, to get rid of stresses and tensions, to help you find inner peace and calm. And you can swim with the dolphins. This is such special water.

And so you swim and you play, and the healing continues, and will continue, even after you are awake, until perfect healing and perfect peace is reached. And this is not the only time you can come and swim and heal in this special water with the loving dolphins. You can come back as often as you wish, as often as you need—to swim again, to play again, and to feel the powerful healing effects of the crystals imparted to the water, absorbed by your body—until the healing is complete.

Spend a few moments now feeling the powerful healing taking place—feeling your body completely relaxed, free of tension, stress, and tightness. If you need to go deeper, a beautiful breath or two or three will take you much, much deeper—much more relaxed. If you are ever uncomfortable with any memory or experience or feeling, just detach from it: Float above it and watch it from a distance, as if you were watching a movie. If you are still uncomfortable, go back to the beautiful garden and rest there as the healing and the relaxation continue. If you are still uncomfortable, you can even open your eyes and rest where you are. But if you are comfortable, stay with it, feel the healing, pay attention to details, to feelings, to thoughts; be mindful of what it is that you are experiencing in your body, in your mind, or even spiritually. Feel the healing, feel the peace, feel the calm. This is so healthy for you.

And now it is time to leave the water. And so you say good-bye to the dolphins for now, and you begin to walk out of the water. Immediately your body is dry; this is such special water. And you sit on the beautiful beach with your friend or friends for a few moments, and you understand much more now about healing, about relaxation, and about inner peace. You understand more now about stress and tension. You can stop the stress reaction very early, just by breathing so peacefully, so calmly. Just by relaxing all of the muscles. Feeling the tightness and tension leave your body, feeling worries leaving your mind.

You understand that worry does no good—it is only a habit. If you stay mindful, in the present moment, there is never a need to worry. Worry always involves the future or the past. Planning for the future is helpful, but worrying about the future does no good. Learning from the past is very helpful. But worrying about the past does no good either. It is over. And so you understand that to stay in the present moment, to feel the peace, the calm, the awareness, the mindfulness of now—this is where joy is. And in the present moment, worry does not exist.

And now you and your friends arise from the beach. Once again, you feel so light and so peaceful. And you float above the island knowing that you can come back whenever you want, whenever you need.

And now, traveling once again across vast distances of space and time, you come back to the beautiful garden—the garden of peace, serenity, love, and light. And you and your friends, in the garden, you feel your body relaxing even more deeply. And you feel the healing that has taken place and will continue until all disease, all illness, and all stress disappears. You've learned how to let go of muscle tension and tightness . . . and feel the peace that this brings. You have learned that it is not necessary to worry. You can feel yourself letting go of all stress-related physical, psychological, and spiritual effects. Your muscles are relaxed, and your breathing is calm. Your stomach is healing . . . your heart. Your pulse is fine, relaxed. There is no need in this state to feel any negative thoughts or emotions. These only harm you.

And so let go of worries, of anxieties, of tension, of stress—you do not need these anymore. They only get in your way. They are obstacles to your inner peace and joy and happiness. And let go of sadness and depression and guilt. You are immortal, you are eternal—and so are your loved ones. You are a soul—not just a body or a brain—and you can never be harmed, not at this level. You are never alone; you are always loved. And we are never really separated from our loved ones. They are always around.

And let go of anger and frustration; these only get in your way, also. They block you. And as you let go of negative thoughts and feelings and emotions, you become aware that underneath these exists a beautiful state of peace, calm, love, and serenity. This is your true inner nature, this is your true core—your inner being. And whenever you want, whenever you wish, you can reconnect to this inner core of peace and love, of compassion, of tranquility. This is your true state. As you let go of anger and frustration, as you let go of fear (there is nothing to fear; you are immortal), as you let go of sadness and guilt and depression, as you let go of worries and tensions and stress, you will always find this inner core of peace and love. This is always within you. This is yours—nobody can take this from you. This is deep within your inner being.

Soon it is time to return for now. But whenever you need to feel this peace again—this calm, this relaxation, this understanding—you can go within once again through your breathing—relaxing your muscles, filling yourself with the beautiful light, surrounding yourself by the light, traveling to the healing island, or even just staying in the beautiful garden, feeling the peace, the recuperation, the healing, that exists all around you. You can come back as often as you want—getting rid of stress, tension, and all of the negative effects. And the more that you practice, the deeper and deeper you will go—even more quickly, even more deeply—reaching that beautiful level of peace and calm, letting go of stresses and tensions, healing your body, healing your mind, restoring your spirit. This is so healthy for you.

Now it is time to return to full waking consciousness. And I will bring you back by counting up from one to ten. With each number up, you will be more and more awake, more and more alert, in full control of your body and your brain, feeling wonderful, feeling great, remembering everything. One, two, three—gently awakening now, more and more alert, more awake; in complete control of your body, of your brain—four, five, six—more and more awake—seven, eight—nearly awake now, feeling wonderful, so peaceful and so calm and yet in full control of body and brain—nine, *ten.*

Open your eyes, stretch if you feel like it—you are completely back, awake and alert, in full control of your body and your brain, feeling wonderful.

about the author

Brian L. Weiss, M.D., is America's leading authority on past-life regression therapy and the author of multiple books, including the *New York Times* bestseller *Many Lives, Many Masters.* As a traditional psychotherapist, he was astonished and skeptical when one of his patients began recalling past-life traumas that seemed to hold the key to her recurring nightmares and anxiety attacks. His skepticism was eroded, however, when she began to channel messages from "the space between lives" that contained remarkable revelations about Dr. Weiss's family and his dead son. Using past-life therapy, he was able to cure the patient and embark on a new, more meaningful phase of his own career.

A graduate of Columbia University and Yale Medical School, Dr. Weiss is also chairman emeritus of psychiatry at the Mount Sinai Medical Center in Miami. He conducts national and international seminars and experiential workshops as well as training programs for professionals.

For more information, please contact
www.brianweiss.com.

Hay House Titles of Related Interest

YOU CAN HEAL YOUR LIFE, the movie,
starring Louise Hay & Friends
(available as a 1-DVD program, an expanded 2-DVD set,
and an online streaming video)
Learn more at www.hayhouse.com/louise-movie

THE SHIFT, the movie,
starring Dr. Wayne W. Dyer
(available as a 1-DVD program, an expanded
2-DVD set, and an online streaming video)
Learn more at www.hayhouse.com/the-shift-movie

* * *

Control Stress by Paul McKenna

*Destressifying: The Real-World Guide
to Personal Empowerment, Lasting Fulfillment,
and Peace of Mind* by davidji

F**K It: Be at Peace with Life, Just as It Is
by John C. Parkin

*A Little Peace of Mind: The Revolutionary
Solution for Freedom from Anxiety,
Panic Attacks and Stress* by Nicola Bird

All of the above are available at your local bookstore,
or may be ordered by contacting Hay House (see next page).

* * *

We hope you enjoyed this Hay House book. If you'd like to receive our online catalog featuring additional information on Hay House books and products, or if you'd like to find out more about the Hay Foundation, please contact:

Hay House, Inc., P.O. Box 5100, Carlsbad, CA 92018-5100
(760) 431-7695 or (800) 654-5126
(760) 431-6948 (fax) or (800) 650-5115 (fax)
www.hayhouse.com® • www.hayfoundation.org

———

Published in Australia by: Hay House Australia Pty. Ltd.,
18/36 Ralph St., Alexandria NSW 2015
Phone: 612-9669-4299 • *Fax:* 612-9669-4144
www.hayhouse.com.au

Published in the United Kingdom by: Hay House UK, Ltd.,
The Sixth Floor, Watson House, 54 Baker Street, London W1U 7BU
Phone: +44 (0)20 3927 7290 • *Fax:* +44 (0)20 3927 7291
www.hayhouse.co.uk

Published in India by: Hay House Publishers India,
Muskaan Complex, Plot No. 3, B-2, Vasant Kunj, New Delhi 110 070
Phone: 91-11-4176-1620 • *Fax:* 91-11-4176-1630
www.hayhouse.co.in

———

Access New Knowledge.
Anytime. Anywhere.

Learn and evolve at your own pace
with the world's leading experts.

www.hayhouseU.com